THE COMPLETE YOU

****

Discover How to be Whole

Don Babin

Copyright 2017 Don Babin.

All rights protected under federal copyright laws. This publication may not be duplicated, copied, or reproduced in any form except by the express permission of the author/publisher, Don Babin.

Book design Copyright © 2017. All rights reserved.

Revival Waves of Glory Books & Publishing

PO Box 596

Litchfield, IL 62056

https://www.revivalwavesofgloryministries.com/

Published in the United States of America

Paperback: 978-1-68411-430-6

Table of Content

Introduction	5
Becoming Whole	8
Wholeness = Peace	17
Wholeness = Integrity	20
Wholeness = Good Attitude	28
Wholeness = Spiritual Warfare	37
Wholeness = Change	43

Forward

This book was birthed from seeing so many struggling believers. It seemed that many really loved Jesus and wanted to serve him, yet something held them back from that real abiding relationship that God desires. As a pastor for over ten years at that time, I wanted to help these people be all God wanted them to be. Some were held back by physical problems, some by emotional problems, and some by spiritual problems. I soon discovered that those who struggled in even one of these areas would find it hard to be victorious in the other areas.

Perhaps you are like some of these. It is my prayer that you find the area that is causing you to miss out on the blessings God has for you. This book will help you to discern areas and bring it in line with the Word of God. Remember this: God loves you and wants to bless you more than you can ever imagine. Make sure that you take your time reading this book and take the time to look up the verses. This should be read in a very prayerful state of mind. If you take this book to heart, I am sure you will see victory, blessings, and peace like never before. God bless you, and I pray to hear from you as to how God has used this study to change your life.

Don Babin

Introduction

In the beginning God created the entire universe and all that it contains by simply speaking them into existence. But it is interesting to note that when He was ready to create man, He became more personally involved, making the creation of man very unique and special. Man was God's grand finale.

He said in Genesis 1, verse 26, *"Let us make man in our likeness..."* revealing at this time that He was not alone in this great plan. Through study of the scriptures, we find that God is three....God, the Father, God, the Son, and God, the Holy Spirit. This revelation of God, which is portrayed throughout scripture, lets us know that He is a Trinity, a trichotomy. Since we are made in the likeness of God, in His image, we are also a trichotomy, made up of three parts.

We find these three parts of man spoken of repeatedly in the Word of God as body, soul, and spirit. At the time of creation, God made man's body from "the dust of the earth" (Gen. 2:7). Then He breathed into this lifeless form "the breath of life" and he "became a living being", receiving at this time a soul and a spirit. We were not just spoken into existence as the rest of His creation. We were God-breathed, into existence!

Our bodies are just "earth suits" to house our spirit and soul. Our spirit and soul live inside this "earth suit". Another way of saying this is that we are jars of clay...

"But we have this treasure in earthen vessels, that the excellence of the power may be of God and not of us".

We find this in 2 Cor. 4:7. Our bodies can become a showcase for these great treasures as we allow God to direct us and change us.

Our soul, is that part of us that God created to give us a free will, free to choose right or wrong. Our soul is our personality, our mind, our will, our emotions.

Our spirit is that part of us that God created when He breathed His life into us. He intended for our spirit to be His habitation, His dwelling place within us. Through man's disobedience in the Garden of Eden, the spirit part of man died to spiritual fellowship with God, and can only have life again through Jesus Christ, through being "reborn". Death simply means separation. Man was separated from the life of God. This is why the bible says, 'the day you eat of it you shall die'. When they ate of the forbidden fruit, they were immediately separated from the life of God. So to receive this life back, we must be 'born another time, or again, of the Spirit of God.

God's plan for us is that these three parts function together as a healthy unit, fulfilling His will in our lives. When any one of these three is not performing as it should, then we are out of balance and not reaching the full potential that God has planned for us.

God intends for us to live life to the fullest. He wants us to enjoy a healthy life, *physically, spiritually,* and *psychologically.* When all three of these work together we reach the summit of how God wants us to live. These three building blocks must be balanced and strong so that we can get everything out of life God planned for us. These building blocks can be looked at like a three legged milking stool. If just one of these legs is not the same as the others in strength or in length, then the stool is out of balance and unstable. This same principle applies to our life. We must be balanced in our spiritual life, psychological life, and physical life. Each of these affects the other. Please understand that this is not some new age concept on 'holistic health', but it is a theological truth on `whole-istic' living.

As you read this booklet, you will learn more about who you are, and how your body, soul, and spirit interact as a unit. This will enable you to correct those things that are out of balance, and strengthen those things that are weak. This will enable you to be all that your Heavenly Father wants you to be in the Kingdom of God. This can be the beginning of you living like you have never lived before.

Becoming Whole

May God Himself, the God of peace, sanctify you through and through. May your whole spirit, soul, and body be kept blameless at the coming of our Lord Jesus Christ.
1 Thes. 5:22

The above scripture shows us that God is very interested in every part of man. If we are to attain our full potential in Christ, and reach fullness God has planned for us, we must learn some basic facts. Each of these three parts mentioned in 1 Thessalonians needs to be meticulously cared for in order to operate properly. Each of these three parts has an effect on one another. If one is not functioning properly, neither is the other two. Because of this basic fact it will be almost impossible to separate these teachings into three categories. We will, however, show the relationship that each have to the function of the other.

Although there are three parts of man; spirit, soul, and body, we need to begin with the spirit. Unless the spirit of man is made alive by the Spirit of God, there is no way that a person can be spiritually healthy. The spirit is that part of man that was made for God's dwelling place. At our physical birth, we receive the breath of life, the spirit placed within the body. This spirit brings life to the body and causes us to breath, have life in the flesh, but since the fall of man in the garden, it is not alive to God. The first thing that has to happen to a person in order to be made whole in his spirit is that his spirit has to experience new birth. This new birth can only come when a person is drawn by the Holy Spirit of God, repents of his/her sins, and asks Jesus to become his/her Lord and Savior. This has to happen to every person, just as it happened to me in the early 1979's.

Drug addiction, rebellion, alcohol, crime and hatred are just a few of the words that described me before I met Jesus. I grew up in the hippie generation and fell right into that trap. For several years all I cared about was being high. There was a huge vacuum inside of me that could not be satisfied with anything the world offered. Sadly it took my trying most of what the world said would make me happy. But through a good friend, I heard the gospel for the first time. Facing a trial with the possibility of several years in the penitentiary, I was finally ready to listen. It was at this time that the biggest miracle of all time happened to me, I was redeemed. I was born another time in the Spirit. That's right, I was born again. Though there have been many trials and hard times since then, I would never undo that decision that transformed my life and future. If you have never been born of the spirit of God, the only way to spiritual health is for you to allow Jesus to take charge of your life, just like I did. At this time you will become a new creation, all things will become new (2 Cor. 5:17). Then you will be ready to start the journey to being made whole in Christ.

At the new birth the spirit is made whole and new. However, at this point, our spirit is just like a newborn baby. In order for us to remain healthy in spirit we must grow spiritually. In order for us to grow spiritually our spirit must be fed and nurtured constantly. Here, then is the first obstacle that a person may face. The "spirit may be willing but the flesh is weak". The spirit wants to read the word, go to church, pray daily, but the soul (intellect, will, and emotions) may not want to do it as often. It is at this point that the baby Christian needs the encouragement and help of the other brothers and sisters in order to keep growing and maintaining spiritual growth. At one time or another we have all been in an unhealthy spiritual state and needed healthy saints to encourage us. Spiritually sick people need a spiritual hospital where, more mature saints, can care for us. Let's not wait until we, or other saints, need spiritual ICU!

It is quite possible for a person to be fairly healthy in one of these three parts, while not being so healthy in the other two. Take, for instance, the body. You may work out at the gym, run or take regular walks, eat only healthy foods, and because of this you are maintaining a fairly healthy body.

Some of you may consider yourself emotionally healthy, healthy in your soul. You are not burdened down with bombarding thoughts of condemnation and guilt. You are not in bondage to fear or worry. You don't have anxiety attacks. You don't allow depression to cripple you. As a whole, you don't carry around unhealthy emotions that could pull you down and hinder you in your service in the kingdom of God. Perhaps you keep a healthy soulish life, by reading books, studying something, challenging yourself with something new.

Some of you may consider yourself to be healthy in your spirit. You are reading the Word and feeding your spirit man. You are communing with the Father through prayer and fasting. You are worshipping God in Spirit and in truth. Your spirit man is in fairly good shape as you maintain these disciplines (in grace) regularly.

It is not enough, however, to pay attention to one of these three parts while neglecting the health of the other two. It is not enough to even try to keep two parts healthy and neglect the third. God shows us clearly in His word that He wants us to be made whole and healthy in every area of our life.

We have only to look around in average church circles to discover that not all Christians are whole in all three of these areas. When I was a pastor I wanted to see the body of Christ have healthy bodies, healthy souls, and healthy spirits. This constitutes a whole person...W-H-O-L-E. The bible talks about wholeness. The whole person includes all three of these vital components. The bible talks about men who served God wholly...body, soul, and spirit.

In the body of Christ today, we find too many who are trying to serve the Lord with a healthy spirit, but are abusing their physical bodies. They are overeating, not eating enough, not eating the right kinds of food, not getting enough exercise, smoking, drinking, taking drugs, and regularly abusing their bodies. We cannot wholly serve the Lord while we are abusing our bodies!

Upon further observation we can find those who may not be abusing their bodies, but are constantly complaining, worrying, speaking negatively, and are generally depressed and unhappy. They may even go to church regularly, but still cannot overcome these attitudes that cause their soul life to be distressed and very unhealthy. When these attitudes and sins of the soul prevail, they not only cause the soul to become unhealthy, but will also negatively affect the growth of the spirit. This is not the victorious life that God wants His children to live.

It is sad to say, but the body of Christ today is made up of many very unhealthy saints. They are malnourished in spirit, lacking in disciplines for a healthy soul, and most have physical problems to boot. They are not wholly serving the Lord as He desires. This is why the church is struggling so in our day and time. When you have a whole lot of people who are sick in body, soul, and spirit, it keeps the few that are healthy very busy trying to nurse them back to health. And many times, because of the majority being unhealthy, the standard for normal is lowered.

It doesn't take a genius to see that there needs to be some changes taking place. Perhaps each of us have identified some of the areas that we need to allow God to work on and bring about changes that will allow us to become healthier in our spirit, soul, and body.

Watchman Nee said, "A spiritual man is not a man born again, but a man born again and walking in alignment". If we are to walk in alignment with God, we must be sure we are taking care of our body, soul, and spirit.

By now most of you may be thinking, "This must be nearly impossible with my schedule and my lifestyle!"

I promise you it is not nearly as hard as Satan and his little entourage of demons would like you to think. It will take some effort, of course, but the biggest key to walking in alignment with God is to let the Holy Spirit show you the wonderful benefits of walking this way. Why not stop right now and ask your great teacher, the Holy Spirit, to bear witness to your spirit that this is a biblical truth. Once you are enlightened on how wonderful it is to walk in peace with God in this area, you will hunger to apply this truth to your daily lifestyle. I know God will show you.

Remember, there is a process that God will take you through to correct the things that are unhealthy in each area of your life. You did not get this way overnight, therefore don't expect that the remedies will come overnight. A good stew takes time to simmer and absorb all of those tasty ingredients. The same goes for biblical truth. Let it simmer and it will get richer. Remember that God is into marinating not micro-waving.

In 1 Thessalonians 5:23 we read, "May God Himself, the God of peace sanctify you through and through. May your <u>whole</u> spirit, soul, and body be kept blameless at the coming of our Lord Jesus Christ."

This scripture is dealing with the three parts of man. We are made in the image of God. It says in Genesis, chapter one, that God made man in His image and likeness. God is a Trinity, God, the Father, God, the Son, and God, the Holy Spirit. He is three, yet He is one.

A GOOD WAY TO SEE THE TRINITY AS ONE AND NOT THREE IS THIS; 1 + 1 + 1 =3

BUT 1 X 1 X 1 =1

Since we are made in His image, we are a spirit, we are a soul, and we are a body. We are three parts, yet we are one. If we were to remove any one of these parts, we would not be a whole person. So, we are spirit, soul, and body. The theological word for this is the **trichotomy** of man. The Bible teaches from cover to cover the **trichotomy** of man. As we consider this in its right perspective, we begin to understand why God wants us to be whole and healthy in every part of our being. Paul is referring to this in

1 Thessalonians 5:23, "May God Himself sanctify you through and through....May your whole spirit, soul, and body be kept blameless".

In this verse Paul is praying for the church. He is praying that they would be *whole* people. Paul wanted a healthy church. The heart of Paul was to be an apostle that planted churches with healthy people. He wanted people to be whole, not part. He wanted them to be whole in their spirit, in their soul, and in their body.

If we are to serve God with our whole spirit, soul, and body, we need to be healthy in all three areas. The problem with many in the church today is that we concentrate on becoming healthy in one of these areas to the neglect of the others. Some may love God with all their heart, but they are sick in their soul, and/or sick in their body. When any one of these areas is suffering and is not healthy, the other areas are not functioning to their fullest potential.

Take, for instance, the person who neglects to feed his spirit regularly with the Word of God, prayer and taking time to enjoy His presence. This person gradually falls away from communing with God. Before long this person becomes malnourished in spirit. It will become virtually impossible for this person to serve God with all his heart because his spirit is sick. By the same token, a person may neglect the care of his soul, harboring unforgiveness, which in turn causes bitterness, hate, and anger. This person will find that he cannot serve God with all his heart because he has a sick soul. When the spirit of a person is sick, and that same person also has a sick soul, you can be fairly sure that he will soon experience sickness in his body. The three parts of man are so connected that it is impossible for one not to affect the others both negatively and positively.

The Church of the Living God must wake up to the fact that the devil is out to kill, steal, and destroy her by all the schemes he can come up with. These include making emotional wrecks out of God's saints; getting them to hold grudges, getting them to have panic attacks, making them fearful, causing them to worry about everything, causing them to complain, causing them to become bitter, to become critical, and abuse our bodies with food, and other poisons, on and on the list could go. If he can get you trapped in just a few of these things, he will have succeeded in making your soul sick so that you can't be all God wants you to be. The devil will also steal your time to be in the Word, and he will try to distract you when you are talking to God. He will help you think up excuses to skip your quiet time, to spend less time than you had planned. If he can get you to do these things, then he will have succeeded in stunting the growth of your spirit, so that you will be unhealthy in that area. He is also out to destroy your physical health. If he can get you to eat junk food, drink zillions of cokes, eat tons of pizza, eat greasy hamburgers, and truckloads of hot dogs, and not exercise, he will have you trapped sooner or later in a body that is unhealthy. Maybe you don't eat all junk food, and maybe you are not over eating or overweight, but you simply don't get the required amount of rest your body needs to function properly. If the devil can convince you that you don't need that much sleep, he will have made a little inroad into your becoming unhealthy in your body. He will use every trick in the book to destroy your physical health. He will even tell you how cool it is to begin puffing on a cigarette. He may fail to tell you that it will someday destroy your lungs! He takes great delight in destroying a Christian's health to the place where they cannot wholly enjoy God. We, as the Church, must wake up out of our stupor, and war against all these tactics he is using to defeat us!

It is my desire that as we face the facts that are presented in this little booklet, that we will be motivated to seek God's help in bringing about the changes needed to be healthy in our spirit, soul, and body. Then together we can go about the business of winning souls and making healthy disciples!

Wholeness = Peace

2nd Thessalonians 3:16

"Now may the Lord of peace Himself give you <u>peace</u> at all times in every way. The Lord be with you all."

     The Hebrew word for peace is shalom, which means 'to be at ease.' This Hebrew word means the opposite of war. The Greek word for peace is 'Ireene', which means 'harmony' or to 'to come together in harmony.' This Greek word, 'Ireene', comes from the word, 'Iraina', Which means 'to be in health.'

     A healthy body works in harmony with itself. The liver is not fighting with the kidney. The heart is not fighting with the lungs. Each part of a healthy body is in harmony with every other part. Thank God our bodies are cooperating with each other in harmony. Imagine if they did not. The body is "at ease." If the body begins to fight against itself, begins to get out of harmony, it gets "dis-ease". When the body gets *dis-ease*, its parts are not functioning together the way God intended for it to function.

     Our body is a miracle! If you begin to study the DNA of the body, and how all the muscles, blood vessels, heart, and cells work together in harmony, you will see the miracle of God. Our bodies have 37.2 trillion cells, each cell having 19 million, million atoms. All of this, is at ease with each other. This is God's design for the body to be free of *dis-ease* as our Creator originally intended.

Just as the physical body has to be in harmony with itself to be "at ease", the spirit and soul have to work in harmony with the body for the whole person to be "at ease". We cannot expect to attain this peace spoken of in the scripture if our spirit is struggling with our soul, or our soul out of sync with the body, or our body out of sync with the spirit. All of this is causing stress in our body. The bible talks about the spirit warring against the flesh, and the flesh warring against the spirit. This is not "at ease"! This is "dis-ease"! If we are going to have this peace, this harmony in our whole person, then we have to recognize that they are inter-linked. We have already seen that the make-up of a person contains the spirit, the soul, and the body. Remember that man is a trichotomy.

If any one of the three gets out of kilter, the body becomes sick. When the body gets sick, we begin to feel bad in our emotions. This means we begin to feel sick in our soul. If we are sick in our soul because our body is sick, then we begin to feel down in our spirit. They are all so inter-linked that when one part suffers the other parts suffer. When we get into this condition of "dis-ease", we cannot serve God wholly.

It is not the Father's will that we remain in such a state of "dis-ease". His desire is that we become a whole people. He desires that we find Shalom, (peace). Since man's fall, he has been at war with God, and with himself. Jesus came to stop the war! He came to bring peace! The angels sang 'peace on earth, good will towards men…."Ireene"!' Jesus came to bring wholeness! Our Lord bought this peace for us at Calvary. He suffered every "dis-ease" in all three parts of His being, that we might obtain this peace, be "at ease" in every part of our being. He gave

His life that we might have life, and have it more abundantly! If we are to become whole people and wholly serve God, we must begin to allow Him to show us where we are lacking, and what we need to do to correct it. When we become healthy in our body, healthy in our soul, and healthy in our spirit, we will then begin to enjoy the abundant life.

We will be people that have *'shalom'*, people that are living in `Ireene'* with God. We will then become a healthy church walking in the Spirit. At this point we will begin to see the manifested presence of God, because God is looking for whole people whom He can flow through.

Wholeness = Integrity

Integrity is a very interesting word, and in this chapter we will explore the way that it is included in the concept of becoming a whole person. The word integrity comes from the mathematical word, "integer". An integer is a whole number. A fraction is a part of a number. An example of this can be found in examining metals, such as steel. When a person asks about the integrity of steel, he is asking if that metal is pure steel. Is it completely steel, wholly steel, or is it mixed with something else? If anything else is mixed with that steel, it loses integrity. The same can be said of a person who is healthy in spirit, soul, and body. We can say that that person is whole. We can also say that that person has integrity. He or she has maintained that integrity by not allowing things to enter his/her spirit, soul, or body that would compromise that integrity.

In the majority of churches we do not see this kind of integrity. Because there is no integrity in the churches in America today, we have become a fragmented body. The only way back to wholeness is through the way that we spoke of in the chapter before this one. Remember that we said Jesus came to stop the war and give us peace. He is stopping the war, and bringing "ease" in place of "disease". He is bringing complete salvation, wholeness, back to the church, His body. When Jesus came to the earth, He was given the title of Prince of `Ireene,' Prince of Peace! He is the only one who can bring integrity into our spirit, soul, and body.

Jesus made provision for His body, the church, to walk in integrity through complete salvation given to every believer. Salvation is a Biblical word. The Greek word for salvation is "sozo.' 'Sozo' means to be made whole. This is what salvation does! It makes a person completely whole! Thank God for His wonderful grace that includes provision for every part of man.

Many evangelical Christians think that salvation means that Jesus only saves our spirit, and that's all. Through examining the scripture, we find that this is in error. In 1 Thessalonians 5:23 we read this: ***"May God Himself, the God of Peace, sanctify you through and through. (Sanctify your body, soul, and spirit.) May your whole body, soul and spirit be kept blameless at the coming of the Lord."***

Once again we find that God is interested in the whole person. Each of us must allow the Holy Spirit to help us grasp this concept of being made whole through this complete salvation. If we do not embrace this concept and allow the Holy Spirit to help us grow in this truth, we will become fragmented in our walk with the Lord, and our integrity will become compromised.

In the next paragraphs we will examine how this `so great salvation' affects our spirit, soul, and body. As was mentioned earlier, the function of each one affects the function of one or both of the other. It is almost impossible to separate them, with any clarity, but we will attempt to give some examples of each. When necessary and appropriate, we will also describe the way one affects the other.

Let's begin with the spirit of a person. God created man with a spirit that had a perfect relationship with His Spirit. This relationship was broken in the Garden of Eden when Adam and Eve sinned by disobeying God. At salvation we are re-united with Him and restored to the place of fellowship with God that was intended in the beginning. We are now one again, made one spirit with His Spirit! 1 Cor. 6:17 *But he who unites himself with the Lord is one with him in spirit.* We read in Genesis that Adam and Eve walked and talked with God. This is how it becomes after salvation. Once again we are able to walk and talk with God. We can come into His presence just like they did in the Garden of Eden!

God is also very interested in our physical bodies. He made provision for our physical bodies to be made whole in this complete salvation.

1 Corinthians 6: 19-20 "Do you not know that your body is a temple of the Holy Spirit, who is in you, whom you have received from God? You are not your own; you were bought at a price. Therefore honor God with your body."

In the above verses we learn that we have received our body from God. At salvation we make Jesus Lord of all, therefore He is Lord of our body. We were bought with a very expensive price therefore we need to honor God with our bodies. To honor Him with our bodies means that we are going to make right choices when it comes to what we put into our bodies. We can begin to walk in integrity where our bodies are concerned if we ask the Holy Spirit's guidance and do the practical things He is telling us to do. Most of us know what foods are healthy and what foods are not. If we need to learn more in this area there are countless numbers of helps available to us today in the form of books, cd's, etc.

Since God emphatically points out that our body is the physical temple of the Holy Spirit, He will help us find the way to make this temple a most attractive place for Him to dwell. He will help, but we must cooperate with Him, and make right choices every day! I point this out because we are all bombarded every day with temptations to make wrong choices. We pick up a magazine or turn on the television and all the alluring ads try to draw us into making bad choices where our bodies are concerned. It is a proven fact that we are poisoning our bodies by what we are consuming. Our food is filled with preservatives, called formaldehyde and monosodium glutamate, growth hormones and this does not include GMO's. Our bodies were not created to consume these things. We consume artificial coloring, fertilizers, growth hormones, pesticides, and we wonder why we have allergies and why our kids have A.D.D. and other dis-eases.

In our nation, young girls are reaching puberty at the ages of eight, nine, and ten years of age instead of thirteen or fourteen as was the case fifty years ago. This is because of the growth hormones we pump into our chicken, and other foods to make them grow larger before slaughtering and then make more profit. We are offering up our kids and our lives on the altar of profits.

We also find that other foods are drastically altered before they are offered to us for consumption. The beef we eat today is being tenderized on the hoof with injections of formaldehyde and antibiotics. Our flesh is soaking up poisons that our liver cannot filter out because the quantity is so great. The foods that we are eating have no nutritional value after we cook it, and microwave it. Some of the foods we consume even our pets refuse to eat it.

We are killing ourselves as a nation with our diet. In 1940 we were the #1 healthiest nation in the entire world. In the 1990's we had dropped to #100. These statistics are proven by the fact that the average American is not healthy in body. Every thirty four seconds someone in America dies from a physical problem associated with heart disease which is brought on by excessive stress, pressure, wrong attitudes and unhealthy diets. Doctors prescribe two billion dollars worth of drugs per year to fight high cholesterol alone. A trillion dollars a year is spent to treat the physical and emotional illnesses in our country.

Other statistics show that adults in America are lacking in several important nutrients. Adult females fail to meet the recommended dietary allowance of five important nutrients: Calcium, vitamin E, vitamin B6, magnesium, and zinc. Adult males failed to meet three nutrients: Magnesium, vitamin E, and zinc. Magnesium is a natural muscle relaxer. If we were getting enough of this vitamin maybe we wouldn't have as many headaches and neck problems.

Two out of three adults in America are overweight. 70.7% of all adult males are overweight. 58.8% percent of all females are overweight. America is now the fattest country in the world. 80% of all Americans do not get the recommended exercise. It is no surprise that we are ranked #100 in the line-up of healthy nations.

One in three Americans will develop cancer in their lifetime. Cancer is killing children between the ages of 13 and 14 like never before in history.

On top of having a poor diet, people in this country also are filling their bodies with drugs, alcohol and tobacco. This is causing cancers and sickness in our bodies and then we want to get mad at God and blame Him. Christians and non-Christians suffer the same consequences for making wrong choices as to the things we put into our bodies. If we do not have integrity where our bodies are concerned we will suffer the consequences.

All of these facts just presented should wake us up as Christians, to want to do something about restructuring our body to become a healthy temple for God. We would not go out and buy a fancy automobile and then fuel it with junk fuel that has trash in it. We put better fuel in our cars than we do fuel in our bodies. The same is true of our bodies, God's temple. If we put junk fuel in it, it isn't going to run right. Sometimes I think we take better care of our cars than we do our temples!

The reason for some of our bad decisions has to do with the fact that we have poor time management skills. We get frustrated because we don't seem to have enough time to shop for and cook proper foods so we rush to the fast foods places. We eat out so much that we overspend our food budget and extend ourselves financially. Then we have to work more hours so we eat more fast foods. We become like a dog chasing his tail.

When we are caught up in this cycle, we begin to wonder way we are not feeling well. We don't seem to be doing so good mentally or spiritually. We just ate four corn dogs and two tacos and was up all night eating Rolaids! We worked 17 hours five days this week and are going to work the week-end, but we can't figure out why we are so irritable with our children and why they are in such rebellion! Everybody driving to work is as stressed out as possible and wonder why everyone has so much road rage.

Many of our problems stem from a lack of discipline. We have become so undisciplined that we let McDonald's and Taco Bell dictate our diet instead of taking responsibility for our own temple that God has given us. We try to keep up with the Jones by buying bigger houses and bigger cars. This keeps us working 10 to 12 hours per day to pay for them. We need to discipline ourselves to be content with a little less, until such time that we can better afford these things. Lack of discipline in these areas causes us to lose integrity and we cannot become the whole person God wants us to be.

This lack of integrity spills over into the lives of our children. Our teenagers are not getting enough rest and that is one reason they struggle emotionally. They may stay up until 2:00 A.M. in the morning doing homework. They may decide to go and ride around `til wee hours of the morning. Then they try to get up at 6:00 A.M. to get ready for school. Then they wonder why they feel so sluggish, why their minds won't function properly. God made our bodies to get plenty of rest. God himself rested after creating the world to give us an example to live by. We must follow this example in order to have a healthy body.

We have learned the importance of having integrity in the spirit and having integrity where the body is concerned. Now we need to deal with having integrity in the soul. You will remember that the soul is that part of us that God created to give us a free will, free to choose right or wrong. Our soul is our personality, our mind, our will, our emotions. Everything that happens in our soul is directly or indirectly related to what takes place in our body and in our spirit.

The soul is where we have the opportunity to make choices, where we can exercise our will. It is here that we have good thoughts or bad thoughts. It is here that we make good choices or bad choices. Having integrity in our soul depends on what kind of choices we make. Having integrity in the soul largely depends on whether we have a good attitude or a bad attitude. In fact, I feel that the subject of attitude is so important, I am devoting the whole next chapter to this subject. It is my desire that as you study this next chapter that you will begin to understand the importance of having a good attitude to maintain integrity in the whole person.

Wholeness = Good Attitude

Phil 2:5

5 Your attitude should be the same as that of Christ Jesus:

Eph. 4:21-24

22 You were taught, with regard to your former way of life, to put off your old self, which is being corrupted by its deceitful desires; 23 to be made new in the attitude of your minds; 24 and to put on the new self, created to be like God in true righteousness and holiness.

When we think of attitude, we either think of a positive one or a negative one. Our countenance shows the world what kind of attitude we have. Our attitude can make a difference in how we live our Christian life. It doesn't matter if we speak in tongues or can raise the dead, if our attitude is not right our witness to the world will be of no effect. If we consistently display a negative attitude, we will tend to turn people off. On the other hand, positive people are very contagious. We as Christians should strive to have a Jesus attitude, and His attitude was a positive one!

Charles Swindoll says, "The longer I live, I realize the impact of attitude on life. Attitude is more important than facts. It is more important that the past. It is more important than education, money, circumstances, failures, and even more important than success. It is more important than what other people think or say, more important than appearance, than gifted abilities or skills. It will make or break a company, a church, or a home." Attitude is not an easy word to define, but the following definitions will give us some insight into what it means. It is the advance man of our true selves. Our attitude can be our best friend or our worst enemy. Our attitude is more honest and more consistent than our words. Our attitude is our outward look that is based on our past experiences. Our attitude is the thing that repels people from us or draws them to us. Our attitude is the librarian of our past; it is the speaker of the present, and it is the prophet of our future.

It can also be said that our attitude is the window to our soul. Most of the time you can tell how healthy a person's soul is by looking at their attitude. In Matthew 12:34 Jesus is talking to the Pharisees. Jesus reveals what kind of attitude He saw through their window when he says,

"You brood of vipers! How can you being evil speak good things? For out of the abundance of the heart the mouth speaks."

We can all see when someone else has "an attitude". We don't need discernment. It's evident when someone is complaining about the pastor preaching on tithing, or keeping the congregation too long, or whining because the music is too loud, or there aren't enough hymns in the service. We don't have to pray for discernment concerning these people. Their attitude tells us that their soul is sick... and complaining.

There are people who develop a bitter attitude. They say, "I've been wounded! My soul and my emotions got wounded in a divorce. My soul, my emotions got wounded by a rebellious child. My soul, my emotions got wounded by the death of someone I loved. My soul, my emotions got wounded by someone in the church."

When someone is wounded in their soul and chooses to hold on to it, they end up with a very bitter attitude. When others look into their window they see bitterness because that person has a bitter attitude.

There are other people who have an angry attitude. They don't understand life, and they get frustrated and angry. They are angry with God, angry with other people, and even angry with themselves. Why are they so angry? Because life is not going the way they think it ought to go. When things begin to happen to them that they did not plan they get angry. They begin to act just like a little baby. Babies cry and fuss because they want what they want and are not getting it. A baby cries when he/she is hungry, he/she is saying, "FO-O-O-OOOOOD!" If food doesn't come or isn't getting there fast enough the baby cries louder. The baby is saying, "Life isn't working right! I am not winning at this!"

When it is time for a baby to be weaned of the pacifier, the parents say, "You are not getting that pacifier! You are a big boy/girl now! You can cry all you want to but you are not getting that pacifier!" Before it's all said and done the baby gets the pacifier. If you want **Ireene...Shalom**....sleep...you give the baby the pacifier! Some Christians are like these little babies. "I'm not supposed to get a flat...I'm never supposed to run out of gas...I'm a spirit filled Christian!"

You may be a spirit filled Christian, but your car isn't!

"I ran out of gas! I got fired! I'm not supposed to get fired! I'm angry!"

There is your window...There is your attitude... anger.

Another prominent attitude that is not hard to spot is an attitude of fear. Some people live in such a prison of fear that they develop extreme phobias. Their behavior becomes very compulsive. People who are always checking the door to make sure it is locked are compulsive. People who are always washing their hands are compulsive. People who are afraid to go out in public for fear of contact with germs are compulsive. If they ever trusted Jesus, they have now begun to focus more on their fear than on Jesus. They have more faith in their fear than they do in Jesus Christ. The only way that such a person is ever going to be set free is through deliverance, and then they must walk in that deliverance to stay free. Sometimes OCD is food related. I believe medical science will soon prove that a lot of our sickness and *diseases* are coming from eating the poisons that are in our food.

There are other attitudes of fear that are not so extreme, but are nevertheless a hindrance to a healthy attitude. Fearful attitudes paralyzes a person so that they cannot move forward in their Christian walk. This is a scheme of Satan to keep the gospel from being advanced. It is a scheme he uses to keep people miserable and discouraged. This then leads to a loss of hope in living a victorious life. He will use every trick in the book to cause us to be fearful. He causes some to be fearful of intimacy. This fear will keep them from having close, fulfilling and loving relationships. This is just what the devil loves. We as Christians should rise up and declare that we are not going to make the devil happy in any way. We will not give him an inch of room to make us fearful. I have had people tell me, 'wow, you have really made the devil mad'. I always respond, 'that's a good thing, because I never want to make him happy'.

There are even people who have a fear of growing old. What they don't realize is that they are becoming old just worrying about growing old! Personally, I am not going to waste one thought on growing old. If I ever do get "old", I'm going to be one senile, on fire, radical old man!! Then people will be talking about me saying, "That's that old preacher, don't worry about him, he's crazy'.

He still goes into the city preaching the gospel, laying hands on sick people, and praying for their healing. He is always singing and talking about Jesus. Well, he's senile, you know." PRAISE THE NAME OF JESUS!!! It will be a glorious thing! I will have an excuse then. Now they just think I'm nuts. But at least I'm screwed onto the right bolt.

Another attitude that we need to guard against is an attitude of self-righteousness. This attitude is one that the devil particularly likes to try to put on Christians. He gets a person to think "There is nothing wrong with me! It's everybody else's fault!" A self-righteous attitude usually hides behind a religious spirit. It becomes extremely difficult for this type of an attitude to be broken once it gets a hold on a person. A person with a religious spirit is never wrong and maintains an unteachable spirit.

Attitudes such as the ones mentioned and many others which develop in the soul, will most certainly affect the body and the spirit. There are places on the internet today that list "attitudes that cause diseases". The attitudes of jealousy, fear, envy, rage resentment, and hatred are the attitudes that cause acids to increase within the stomach and make a hole in the lining. Excess sorrow, excessive ambition, excessive frustration, worry, loneliness due to a need for love, can lead to serious mental and physical illnesses.

We need to examine ourselves where our attitude is concerned. We need to be willing to change if we find any area of our soul life that needs an attitude adjustment.

As Paul says in the scripture in Ephesians, we need *"to be made new in the attitude of our minds."* This means that we have the choice and privilege to change our minds. The wonderful thing is that we have a choice every day regarding the attitude we embrace for the day.

We cannot change our past. We cannot change other people, but we can change our response to things that happen to us. Life is ten percent what happens to us and ninety percent how we respond. We are in charge of our attitude. We are faced with conflicting situations every day that affects our attitude. Conflict is inevitable, combat is optional. When we are drawn into these kinds of situations, we need to ask Jesus what kind of an attitude He would have in a similar situation. We need to draw our strength from Him. If we maintain a Jesus attitude we will only have conflict and not combat. We will be renewed in the attitude of our mind.

Each of us need an attitude adjustment from time to time. We need to take inventory and let the Holy Spirit show us in what areas we need a change of attitude. The following are a few points that will help you develop a good attitude.

(1) **Never react, only respond.**

Matt 5:11-12

11" Blessed are you when people insult you, persecute you and falsely say all kinds of evil against you because of me. Rejoice and be glad, because great is your reward in heaven, for in the same way they persecuted the prophets who were before you."

When we are insulted it affects our attitude. Nobody wants to be insulted, but when we are, if we will `rejoice and be glad in it', we will be blessed. Jesus is not saying here that when people insult you the Holy Ghost is going to swoop down on you and give you goose bumps. He is not saying that He is going to take control of your mouth and your vocal chords, and you will automatically start blessing that person. You are still going to want to lash back at the person who has insulted you, but you make the choice not to do it. It is not a spiritual experience, it is a choice. When you make the right choices, then you reap blessings. When you make wrong choices, you will reap crummy results!

If you rejoice inside and are exceedingly glad when someone insults you, you will reap the benefits. High blood pressure, stress, and ulcers are what you will reap if you make the wrong choice and react with resentment and anger. Peace, joy, and blessings come when we obey.

When we take medication and we 'react' to it, we usually get hives or an upset stomach. When we `respond' to medication, it means we are getting well. The medication is working. The Spirit of God will help us make the choice to respond, and He will enable us to follow it through. He will not swoop down and make it happen in your life. You have to choose to not *react,* but to *respond.*

(2) *We* **need to look at things from God's perspective.**

Rom 8:28

28 And we know that in all things God works for the good of those who love him, who have been called according to his purpose. It

When you are going through a tough situation, you can look at it from your perspective, and the world can fall apart. You can have a giant pity-party and begin thinking that nothing in your life is worth living anymore. You can believe that God doesn't love you and has abandoned you Or you can say, "My God Reigns! Everything that happens in my life is filtered through Jesus Christ! I know what is going on in my life is tough. I don't understand it, but I accept it, and I know that Jesus is right by my side going through it with me!" I love the verses in the Bible that remind us, 'It came to pass…'. Why did it come? TO PASS! It just came so it could pass.

We don't need to be asking, "Why?" God does not owe us any answers. We just need to have faith and accept the fact that God is sovereign. When bad things happen, it doesn't mean that God has abandoned us. It doesn't mean that He is mad at us.

When you look at everything from your own perspective, it is showing a selfish attitude. If you completely take yourself out of the picture and look at how big God is, you will develop the right attitude. Don't focus on the size of your problems but the size of your God.

We should develop the attitude that says, "My God is all knowing. My God is all powerful. My God deeply loves me. He chose me, He adopted me, He forgave me, He accepts me, and He cares about me. God is in charge of whatever is going on in my life and I am going to praise Him for it!"

(3) We need to let people help us.

Eccl 4:10

If one falls down, his friend can help him up. But pity the man who falls and has no one to help him up!

We all need help with our attitude occasionally. The reason most of us won't let other people help us is because we don't want them to see what a crummy attitude we have. I have news for you, they already see it! We may be afraid of what they will think of us.

We don't want to face the truth about ourselves, so we just choose to hide from it, and think that we are okay, and it is everybody else that has the problem. If this is the way you are thinking, this is for you, because there is no one who has arrived. We are all working towards the mature Christian life.

We have learned that our attitude is the window of our soul, but it is hard to look into our own window. We may be quick to see others displaying a bad attitude, but fail to see the same thing in ourselves. Here is some good advice concerning this. Find someone whom you love and trust and hold each other accountable. Be honest with each other and hold each other accountable in the area of your attitudes. There are a lot of people looking into our window checking our attitude. We need to walk in integrity so that we can be a Christ like witness.

Wholeness = Spiritual Warfare

We should never forget as Christians that we are constantly engaged in spiritual warfare. This war takes place in the overall body of Christ, but it also takes place in each individual child of God. The devil is out to "steal, kill, and destroy" every one of us. He doesn't play fair, nor does he care that we may not be aware of his schemes. God sent Jesus to "destroy the works of the devil (1 John 3:8)" and "give us life more abundant (John 10:10)." This then is the battle that is raging. God wants us to live an abundant life, but the devil wants to destroy what God is doing.

There are several words for "life" in the Greek language. "Bios" is one of these words, and this is where we get the word, biology. Biology is the study of physical life. Biology would include the study of man's **body**.

Another Greek word for life is "Psych**e**". This is where we get the word, psychology. This study is about the behavior of man that takes place in the **soul**. The soul is the place in man that allows for free will. It includes the mind and emotions.

The Greek word, "Zoe" is the life of God, or **Spiritual life**. When we read the word, life, in the New Testament, the majority of the time it is "zoe". "Zoe" life, eternal life, is not a sense of quantity. It is not talking about longevity. It is talking about the quality of life. God breathed this "zoe' life into man in the garden. When man sinned God withdrew His Spirit and took "zoe' away. All of a sudden man lost his sense of purpose. "Why am I here? Why was I born?" Now man has become futile in his thinking. Everything begins to be centered around him.

It is interesting to note that the three words for life includes the study of all three areas of our makeup, **body**, **soul**, and **spirit**. Since God wants us to have abundant life, He has surely made provision for us to be victorious in all three; body, soul, and spirit.

Let us go back to the garden, and see what God did there. God became a sculptor and sculpted a man, but it had no life. Man was like a statue. God walked up to this statue and literally breathed the breath of life into him. The word, breath, in the Greek is "pnuma". It is where we get the word, pneumonia and pneumatic. This word speaks of air or pneumatic tools, tools driven by air. Many times in the New Testament the Holy Spirit is referred to as 'wind' or `air'.

John 3:8

8" The wind blows where it wishes, and you hear the sound of it, but cannot tell where it comes from and where it goes. So is everyone who is born of the Spirit..."

When God breathed His breath of life into man, man received his soul, his personality, his temperament, his ability to choose. Nothing else in the universe can choose. A bird doesn't choose. An animal doesn't choose. They are plugged into God's computer called instinct. They do what God programmed them to do. Man, on the other hand, used to live in caves, but now builds eighty story buildings because he chooses to do so. Not even the angels can choose.

When a person begins to feel the wind of the Holy Spirit blowing into his life, he is given a choice. His soul comes into play at this time, and he can choose heaven or hell. He can choose life or death. He has the choice. The Holy Spirit is tugging at his spirit to make the right choice, but the person himself has to make the choice. God has given man a very unique ability that nothing else in creation has; a free will, the ability to choose.

If, at this time, the person chooses Jesus as his Lord, he is given a new birth. God at this time places His Holy Spirit inside of that person and he receives new life, "Zoe".

Every part of this person's life is about to change. "Bios", his body life, is going to change. Instead of a sad countenance, he will now have a smile. Instead of going through the motions of worship, he will now dance and shout because he is a new creation, a new man. His psyche, his soul, is going to change. His soul has gotten the message from his spirit that it is now alive, and the soul has sent the message to his body, and his body can no longer stand still! All three parts are now experiencing change, and this makes the devil mad! The bible says we become a peculiar people, and the devil doesn't hesitate to tell the world that we are crazy. This should be viewed as a compliment to the new Christian. He is now a light in the world of darkness.

When we are born again we become a new creation in Christ Jesus.

2 Cor. 5:17

17 Therefore, if anyone is in Christ, he is a new creation; old things have passed away; behold, all things have become new.

This does not mean that we are never going to have a battle. This does not mean that we will never again be tempted to sin. This does not mean that we will never yield to temptation. On the contrary, the battle has just now begun. My spirit man (new man) which is now joined with God's Spirit wants to be the controlling factor in my spiritual life. But I soon find out that there is another part of me, my flesh (the old man), that rises up and tries to dictate to my soul and get me to make wrong choices.

Now the choice is up to me. If I am reading and meditating on the word of God, I can say, "By the word of God, what I am doing is wrong and I know it is wrong." Then my will has to say, "I submit to the Spirit of God which is joined to my spirit," or I submit to my flesh (the old man) and do what I feel like doing.

This battle of self will, must be fought and won over and over in our Christian walk. The Spirit of God resides in us and is teaching us how to overcome the devil in these battles. Each time we resist him and draw nearer to God we become stronger. On the other hand, if we continue to yield to temptations, giving way to the enemy of our soul, we will not experience the spiritual growth that God desires for us. The way to defeat the devil in this battle of self will is brokenness. Brokenness is not necessarily tears. Brokenness is when your will is broken from what you want to do to what God wants you to do. "Not my will but thy will be done" is brokenness. This takes place in our soul.

Another battle that the enemy loves to get us caught up in is the battle of self-worth. If he can convince us that we are no good, that we are worthless, that we'll never make it as a Christian, he will win the battle. He works on all of us at one time or another in this area. I get up some days and I don't feel a bit spiritual. I feel like the devil. My wife sometimes says I act like him. That doesn't mean that I am unspiritual. It is purely a feeling. I am what the word of God says I am. I am the righteousness of God. Jesus shed His blood for me. I am blameless before God because of His blood. We need to live and act like what the word of God says about us, and not what our feelings are telling us. Feelings are very unreliable, therefore we must not trust them, but instead trust God's word.

It is important to equip ourselves by studying God's word before the enemy attacks so that we will have something with which to fight the battle. The word of God is the sword of the Spirit, but we must read it, learn it, hide it in our heart in preparation for battle. Only the Word of God has the ability to cut between the soul and the spirit.

Heb. 4:12

12 *For the word of God is living and active. Sharper than any double-edged sword, it penetrates even to dividing soul and spirit, joints and marrow; it judges the thoughts and attitudes of the heart.*

Another battle that we will at one time or another find ourselves engaged in is the battle of pride. We may think we are doing pretty good in our spiritual walk. We may even begin to feel like we've reached great spiritual heights. If we get our eyes off Jesus, and begin to concentrate on what we're doing for him, we begin to allow the enemy to deceive us. We become proud of what we've achieved or done. Someone once said that pride is so deceitful that you can become proud of being humble. God is very displeased with a prideful spirit. In fact, it is listed in Proverbs as one of the things that God hates. Another verse in Proverbs tells us that pride will cause us to fall.

Prov. *16:18 18 Pride goes before destruction, a haughty spirit before a fall.*

The only remedy for pride is humility. If you discover that you are losing in the battle of pride, the only way to be restored is to humble yourself under the mighty hand of God. God is not going to come charging out of heaven, beat you to your knees, and make you humble. He has instructed you to

"Humble yourselves, therefore, under God's mighty hand, that he may lift you up in due time." 1 Peter 5:6

He will lift you up by giving you grace. God gives grace to the humble. You don't get grace if you are proud.

James 4:6

"God opposes the proud, but gives grace to the humble."

HUMILITY is not thinking less of yourself but thinking of yourself less. You might want to read that again.

God never wanted robots. He could make man do whatever He wants because He is God. But He wants us to choose Him over everything else. He wants us to walk in the Spirit, and not fulfil the lusts of the flesh.

Our Heavenly Father is a good God, a good Father. He wants the very best for us. Let's become the whole people that He desires. Let's live a spirit filled life. Let's live blamelessly until the coming of Christ in our spirit, in our soul, and in our body.

Wholeness = Change

Luke 2:51-52 And Jesus grew in wisdom and stature, and in favor with God and men.

In this scripture in Luke, we see a perfect example in the person of Jesus as to how change should take place in every area of our physical and spiritual existence. We see that Jesus grew in wisdom, His soul. We see that Jesus grew in stature, His physical body. We see that Jesus grew in favor with God and man. This speaks of His spirit. Jesus grew spiritually. He had communion with the Father and community with man. From this scripture we can safely say that Jesus changed.

Since Jesus left us such an explicit example, don't you think that He will help us to make changes in our lives to become completely whole in body, soul, and spirit? You may say, "Yes, but Jesus never sinned! He didn't have to overcome all the things I have to face." WRONG! True, Jesus never sinned, but Jesus faced exactly every temptation that you have faced!

Heb. 4:15

For we do not have a high priest who is unable to sympathize with our weaknesses, but we have one who has been tempted in every way, just as we are-yet was without sin.

Not only did he face temptation, he overcame every one without yielding to sin. He can help us do the same. He can help us to make the necessary changes to become whole.

Heb. 2:18 Because he himself suffered when he was tempted, he is able to help those who are being tempted.

Jesus left us a great example. He sent His Holy Spirit to help us. He also has given us explicit instructions in the book called the Bible. With all this help what are we missing? I think that what we are missing is the practical things. The things that can help us live for Jesus in a difficult world. We need practical things about Jesus to apply to our lives to help us with the financial struggles, relational struggles, our job struggles; and our spiritual struggles. We need to know what the bible says about all these situations and areas of our lives. How do I live for Jesus in an extremely difficult world? It is hard to work around people that don't love Jesus and are living their lives contrary to God's word. It's hard to live a spirit filled life around people who talk bad, who tell dirty jokes, and try to get you to listen. This is the kind of world we live in, so how do we live a Christian life in a world filled with this sort of thing?

We can see from all this that change is in order, but what do we do. I'm glad you asked, because I am going to give you some practical things that work, if you do them. It is your responsibility to take what we share with you and apply it to your life.

First, we must learn to take the word of God and practice it. We have to put it into action. I picture the body of Christ today as having great big ears and tiny little feet. We travel from conference to conference, soaking up the sermons, but never putting into action what we supposedly are learning. Big ears, tiny feet, hearing but never walking in it. We go to service after service and hear but never move, never change. We go to church Sunday after Sunday, but we never get rid of our secret sinful lives. Our lives have no discipline. Our marriage doesn't get any better. We are not raising our children to be children of God.

Why go to church if nothing ever changes? We have formed a habit of going to church to get a quick fix; a fix for our depression, a fix for our troubled marriage. We think the preacher will make us feel better about our circumstances. We think the preacher will inspire us right into next Sunday's sermon. We think he can wave a magic wand somehow and fix all our problems. As a preacher I feel like a bicycle pump. You come to church, I pump you up, then you go home and get deflated watching the *"hellevision"*.

No matter how inspired you may feel after a Sunday morning service, it is not going to help you live out the Christian life tomorrow. It may help you feel good for a couple of hours today, but it will not help you live in this world and fight all the battles. You have to do something about what you hear. Change is the name of the game.

Just suppose I went to a fancy restaurant and ordered a steak dinner with a wonderful baked potato, and a healthy side salad. Suppose after my dinner had been brought I just sat and stared at it, taking deep whiff of the aroma. Suppose the waitress asked after a few minutes if everything was O.K. I would say, "Oh, yes! I admire this meal and it is beautiful. It is the best meal I have ever seen. As a matter of fact, if I ate this meal I know it would be nutritious and good for me. I am going to remember this meal for a long time." I can study the meal, memorize the meal, analyze the meal, disagree with the meal, but if I don't consume the meal it will never serve it purpose. Suppose I then just got up and left without ever eating that meal. It would not do me any good whatsoever.

Isn't that the way we do the word of God? It doesn't do any good to gaze at the word, or memorize it if we don't apply it to our lives. We have to live what we hear and read. It has to live in us. We need to take it and consume it just like a meal and let it become part of our life.

If you don't take what is shared with you and study it, consume it, and apply it to your life you have wasted your time. It's just like that meal in the restaurant that I ordered and stared at, but didn't eat. It was wasted. We can go to church and gaze at the meal, memorize the meal, study the meal, have a great revelation of how that meal could change our lives, and never eat the meal.

If you are going to church just to get a good feeling, cocaine and alcohol can do that very same thing for you. The world is looking for a good feeling and that is why we have millions of drug addicts and alcoholics in this nation. People in this nation become addicted to a drug that their own bodies release. Dopamine is a chemical released by your brain that causes a sense of well-being. Pornography releases this chemical in the brain. Those who become addicted to pornography are really addicted to this chemical called dopamine released by their own body. All of these addictions started because of a lack of discipline. The bible talks about sinning against your own body in Corinthians. You can't sin against your own body and then expect a quick fix from God to make you well. Jesus spent a lot of time healing people in His day because He wanted them to be whole. He also said in one instance ***"go and sin no more, lest a worse thing come upon you."***

You may come to church after working ten to fifteen hours a day, eating junk food, staying up all night watching T.V., and then want God to heal you. I wish it were that easy! I can lay hands on you, but if your lifestyle doesn't change, you will be right back where you were in a few weeks. When you are sick and go to the doctor, he gives you an injection that will work immediately. The doctor then writes a prescription for you to take for 10 days. You have to take the rest of the medicine or you will not continue to get better. You have to discipline yourself to take it every day until finished. The anointing of oil or the laying on of hands will help you immediately, but if you don't take the rest of the prescription at home you will not get well. It is the prescription of God's word and the discipline of your life that is going to make you whole. As you apply these things you will be able to walk victoriously on this earth.

We have learned thus far that we all need to change. Change can only come about as we do the things that we learn from God's word. In order to do God's word we have to study God's word. We need to meditate on it, memorize it, and consume it. Then we need to do something about it. In order to do something about it, we are going to have to exercise discipline. When the word is telling us to do something, we need to do it. When the word is telling us not to do something, we need to not do it!

Now we are going to get a little more specific in the ways we need to change. One of the first places that most of us need to exercise discipline and make changes is in the way we treat our body.

1 Cor. 6:19

Do you not know that your body is a temple of the Holy Spirit, who is in you, whom you have received from God? You are not your own; 20 you were bought at a price. Therefore honor God with your body.

Rom 12:1

Therefore, I urge you, brothers, in view of God's mercy, to offer your bodies as living sacrifices, holy and pleasing to God-this is your spiritual act of worship.

In these two passages of scripture God is telling us that we will glorify GOD by taking care of our bodies. He is saying that to take care of our temples (our bodies) is an act of spiritual worship to Him. If God considers our bodies so important, shouldn't we want to do everything we can to keep them healthy?

In the Garden of Eden, Adam and Eve were in perfect health. Adam did not have a pot-belly. It all started with eating the wrong food. God could have said, "Do not climb that mountain." But he chose to relate their first discipline to food.

Since one of the first disciplines in the bible is related to food, we may deduct that God expects us to be disciplined in what we eat, in what we put into our bodies. My first practical suggestion toward having a healthy body is this. Eat healthy. There are a lot of good books out there that can help you in this area. Most of us already know generally what we should and shouldn't eat. The problem lies in discipline again. We must learn to discipline ourselves in what we eat and how much we eat.

The next suggestion is that we get more exercise. Most of us do not get enough exercise in our daily routines. It is again a matter of discipline. We can either do more walking, join a health club and work out, or get an inexpensive piece of equipment that will help us get the needed exercise for our bodies to be healthy. There again, if we get the equipment, and don't use it, it will do us no good.

Another place we need to change is in the amount of rest and sleep we get. We cannot possibly be healthy in body when we are not getting adequate sleep or rest. We shouldn't be up all night watching television or working day and night without sleeping. It is important to God for us to sleep and have adequate rest. He rested one day after creation to set an example for us to follow.

It has been proven that people who have a struggle with physical problems, like losing weight, do better if they are in a support group. Even in studies done with women who have breast cancer, it has been found that those who had a strong support group lived longer over a seven year period and had less chance of relapse. HIV patients progressed slower in their diseases when they had strong friendships according to PHD Marcus Hindrix in the University of Zuric. Church and home cell groups are strong support groups. This is why God tells us not to forsake the assembly of ourselves together. My suggestion, then, is that you get into a strong support group and let other people help you make the changes needed for a healthy body.

Another practical suggestion that has been proven to be beneficial is to learn to laugh a lot! You may wonder how this can help you be healthier in your body. Research has shown that 100-200 deep hee-haws can benefit your body as much as ten minutes of boat rowing. Dr. Fry says that laughing gets your blood circulating, gives your heart a work out, supplies your lungs with oxygen, stimulates your brain, activates your immune system, and suppresses stress hormones. The average preschooler laughs 400 times per day. The average adult only laughs 15 times per day. The bible says in

Prov. 17:22 A merry heart does good, like a medicine, but a broken spirit dries the bones...

We as adults need to learn to laugh more and it will be like medicine to us.

I have one more practical suggestion to make that will not only help you to have a healthier body, but will help you build up your faith. This suggestion is that you pray often, every day, in your heavenly language you received when you were baptized in the Holy Spirit.

Jude 20

But you, dear friends, build yourselves up in your most holy faith and pray in the Holy Spirit.

You may be thinking, "I can see where it would help me to build up my faith, but how can it help me to be healthier in my body?" Being right with God has a direct effect on how you feel physically. Dr. Carl Peterson, a brain specialist with ORU in Tulsa, Oklahoma, was doing research on the brain and praying in tongues. Some amazing things were discovered. As we engage in our heavenly language, the brain releases two chemical secretions that are directed into our immune system, giving us a thirty five to forty percent boost to our immune system. This promotes healing within our bodies. Amazingly this secretion is triggered from a part of the brain that has no apparent activity in humans. This is science talking, not just me! In light of this, it would seem that using our prayer language as often as possible would be very beneficial to a healthier body.

We are responsible for taking care of our temples and teaching our families to do the same. We need to get disciplined about all of these important issues. If we have a healthy body, we will have a healthy soul. If we have a healthy soul, we will be a happy person with a healthy spirit.

I think we can all agree that there are some changes that we can make to become whole in body, soul, and spirit. Pray and ask the Father to reveal to you the adjustments you need to make in your life. Ask Him for the grace to be able to do it. Ask Him to give you the discipline. Ask Him to give you integrity in your life. He will help you because you will be praying according to His will and because he really loves you!

www.ingramcontent.com/pod-product-compliance
Lightning Source LLC
LaVergne TN
LVHW021739060526
838200LV00052B/3368